W9-BAP-522

A Guide for Using

Holes

in the Classroom

Based on the book written by Louis Sachar

*This guide written by **Belinda Zampino** and **Rebecca Clark***

Teacher Created Materials, Inc.
6421 Industry Way
Westminster, CA 92683
www.teachercreated.com
©2000 Teacher Created Materials
Reprinted, 2002
Made in U.S.A.
ISBN 1-57690-650-7

Edited by
Eric Migliaccio

Illustrated by
Bruce Hedges

Cover Art by
Tim Andren

Table of Contents

Introduction

A good book can touch our lives like a good friend. Within its pages are words and characters that can inspire us to achieve our highest goals. We can turn to it for companionship, recreation, comfort, and guidance. It can also give us a cherished story to hold in our hearts forever. In Literature Units, great care has been taken to select books that are sure to become good friends!

Teachers who use this unit will find the following features to supplement their own valuable ideas.

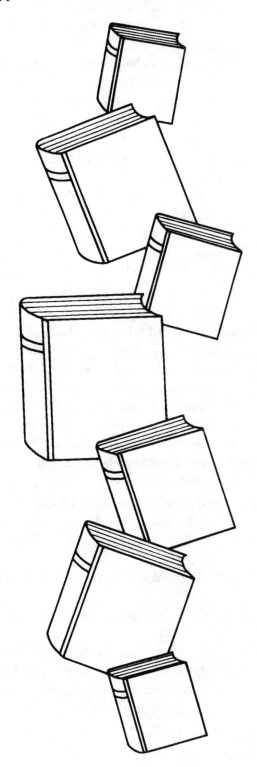

- Sample Lesson Plans

- Pre-reading Activities

- A Biographical Sketch and Picture of the Author

- A Book Summary

- Vocabulary Lists and Suggested Vocabulary Activities

- Chapters grouped for study with each section including the following:

    —quizzes

    —hands-on projects

    —cooperative learning activities

    —cross-curricular connections

    —extensions into the reader's own life

- Book Project Ideas

- Post-reading Activities

- Research Activity

- Culminating Activities

- Three Different Options for Unit Tests

- Answer Key

- Bibliography of Related Reading

We are confident this unit will be a valuable addition to your planning, and we hope your students increase the circle of "friends" they have in books as you use our ideas.

Sample Lesson Plans

Each lesson suggested below may take from one to several days to complete.

Lesson 1: Introduction
- Introduce the novel and complete the pre-reading activities (page 5).
- Read "About the Author" aloud with your class (page 6).
- Present vocabulary for Section 1 and do one activity (pages 8–9).

Lesson 2: Read Chapters 1–7
- Have students write in reading response journals (page 14).
- Build a class model of Camp Green Lake (page 11).
- Have students work with partners to find out nicknames (page 12).
- Research West Texas and local geography (page 13).
- Administer quiz for Section 1 (page 10).
- Present vocabulary for Section 2 and do one activity (pages 8–9).

Lesson 3: Read Chapters 8–17
- Make Camp Green Lake T-Shirts (page 16).
- Have students work with partners to research inventions (page 17).
- Make fossils of classroom objects (page 18).
- Explore future plans (page 19).
- Administer quiz for Section 2 (page 15).
- Present vocabulary for Section 3 and do one activity (pages 8–9).

Lesson 4: Read Chapters 18–28
- Do the spiced peaches activity (page 21).
- Practice cause-and-effect skills with a partner (page 22).
- Do "Are You a Math Whiz?" activity (page 23).
- Conduct a class discussion about illiteracy (page 24).
- Administer quiz for Section 3 (page 20).
- Administer test for Sections 1–3 (page 42).
- Present vocabulary for Section 4 and do an activity (pages 8–9).

Lesson 5: Read Chapters 29–39
- Create brochures to advertise Camp Green Lake (page 26).
- Work with a partner to distinguish fact from opinion (page 27).
- Examine the different types of literary conflicts (page 28).
- Role-play about bullies (page 29).
- Administer quiz for Section 4 (page 25).
- Present vocabulary for Section 5 and do an activity (pages 8–9).

Lesson 6: Read Chapters 40–50
- Organize and present mock trial (page 31).
- Identify characters' traits from *Holes* (page 32).
- Write from different viewpoints (page 33).
- Conduct discussion and write letters about homelessness (page 34).
- Administer quiz for Section 5 (page 30).

Lesson 7: Closure
- Discuss novel with class and make connections (page 38).
- Assign book project and/or research activity (pages 39 and 40).
- Assign "Conversations" (page 41).
- Complete one or more culminating activities (pages 35–37).
- Administer tests for Sections 4 and 5 (page 43) or assign other test options (pages 44 and 45).
- Discuss test answers and recommend related reading (page 48).

Before the Book

Before you begin reading *Holes* with your students, do some pre-reading activities with the class to stimulate and enhance their comprehension. Here are a few activities and discussion questions that might work for your class.

1. Predict what the story will be about just by hearing the title.

2. Discuss other books written by Louis Sachar.

3. Divide students into small groups. Assign each group one of the following questions. Give the groups enough time to discuss their questions. Have each group present their findings to the class. Allow other students to add as each group presents.

   —Have you ever known anyone who was punished for something he didn't do?

   —Have you ever had an experience with a bully?

   —Would you be willing to help someone learn to read?

   —How important is it for you to belong to a group?

   —Would you lie to protect someone else?

   —Do you believe in curses or bad luck?

4. Place each of the following items in front of the class. Instruct students to write down each item as you present and identify it. When their lists are complete, have students predict the role of each item in the story. Students should keep their lists until the end of the unit to check the accuracy of their predictions.

   ❑ sneakers

   ❑ peach preserves

   ❑ sunflower seeds

   ❑ onion

   ❑ lipstick tube

   ❑ fish fossil

   ❑ box of stationery

5. Have students bring in articles about juvenile offenders who have been convicted. Identify the crimes committed and the punishments received. Stimulate class discussion using the following questions:

   —Does the punishment fit the crime?

   —What do you think would be an appropriate punishment?

   —Should juveniles be tried as adults?

About the Author

Louis Sachar was born in East Meadow, New York. When he was nine, he and his family moved to Southern California, and that is where he grew up.

Louis Sachar attended the University of California at Berkeley and worked at Hillside Elementary as a teacher's aide. During his last year as an undergraduate (1976), he began writing. He had always wanted to write, and he didn't like the stories that the students at Hillside Elementary were reading. His first book was *Sideways Stories from Wayside School*, a story about a very strange school. What made the school so strange? It's 30 classrooms were built on top of each other (as opposed to side-by-side); and it employed one teacher, for instance, who liked to turn the students into apples. The book was popular but didn't sell many copies. He decided to attend law school but continued to write on the side.

After passing the California State Bar Exam, he wrote two more books: *Johnny's in the Basement* and *Someday, Angeline*. At first, he didn't know if he wanted to be a lawyer or a writer. He eventually chose his first love, writing.

Louis Sachar met his wife when he showed up for a book signing at Davis Elementary in Plano, Texas. He fell for the school's counselor, Carla Askew. They got married, and Carla convinced him to move to Texas. They now live in Austin with their daughter, Sherre.

Louis Sachar's dislike of the summer heat in Texas gave him the idea for *Holes*. He said that you expect to be hot in July and August, but in Texas the heat just keeps going and going. He decided to write about the oppressive heat and a place where it was impossible to get away from the heat. Sachar said the characters grew out of the place.

Sachar has written 20 books altogether. Some of the titles include *Sideway Stories from Wayside School, The Boy Who Lost His Face, There's a Boy in the Girls' Bathroom, Dogs Don't Tell Jokes,* and the *Marvin Redpost* series. In February of 1999, *Holes* was awarded the Newbery Medal Award. (The Newbery Medal Award, which has been awarded since 1922, is the highest honor given in children's literature in the United States.)

Louis Sachar said that when he writes, he tries to please only one reader: himself. He likes to write books that are fun.

Holes

by Louis Sachar

(Farrar, Strauss and Giroux, 1998)
(available in CAN, Douglas & McIntyre)

While walking home from school one day, Stanley Yelnats is hit over the head with a pair of sneakers that have fallen from an overpass. Stanley is stopped by the police and arrested. It turns out that the sneakers had been stolen from a homeless shelter where they were being auctioned off to raise money. As a result, Stanley is sent to a juvenile detention center.

Camp Green Lake, located in the heat of West Texas, has no lake and is certainly not green. The camp is run by an evil warden. Camp routine requires each "inmate" to dig a five feet wide by five feet deep hole everyday. The counselors tell Stanley that digging builds character, but Stanley becomes suspicious when he is told to turn in anything "interesting" that he digs up.

Stanley blames all his bad luck on his great-great grandfather, Elya Yelnats, who had forgotten a promise to carry an elderly gypsy to the top of a mountain. The gypsy, Madame Zeroni, had cursed Elya and his descendants.

While digging his required hole, Stanley finds a lipstick tube belonging to "Kissin' Kate Barlow," a notorious outlaw. Miss Katherine Barlow, a schoolteacher in Green Lake 110 years ago, had rejected the advances of the wealthy Trout Walker and instead had fallen in love with an onion peddler named Sam (who happened to be black). When the townspeople found out about this love affair, Sam was killed and Katherine was run out of town. Her life destroyed, Katherine became "Kissin' Kate Barlow" and began a robbing and killing spree that lasted 20 years. She eventually returned to Green Lake but died before Trout Walker could force her to reveal the location of the treasure she had amassed over the years.

Stanley agrees to teach one of the other boys, Zero, how to read. This gets both boys into trouble and causes Zero to run away from the camp. Stanley sets out to save Zero. The two boys try to find refuge at the top of a mountain called God's Thumb. Zero becomes ill, and Stanley ends up carrying him to the top of the mountain. "Zero," it turns out, is short for "Zeroni," and Zero is Madame Zeroni's descendant; consequently, the curse is broken.

The boys build their strength by eating the healing onions planted years ago on God's Thumb by Sam the Onion Man. Zero confesses that he is the one who stole the sneakers from the homeless shelter. Stanley and Zero decide to return to camp to look for Kate Barlow's buried treasure. The boys return to the hole where the lipstick tube was found and dig through the night. They dig up a suitcase, which had belonged to the first Stanley Yelnats, but they are descended upon by deadly yellow-spotted lizards and are unable to move. The Warden, a descendant of Trout Walker, discovers the boys and waits for the lizards to finish them off so she can get the briefcase. Stanley's lawyer and the Texas Attorney General show up at the camp and rescue Stanley and Zero. The contents of the suitcase are valuable enough to help Stanley buy his family a home and for Zero to hire private detectives to find his mother, from whom he had been separated.

Vocabulary Lists

On this page are vocabulary lists which correspond to each sectional grouping of chapters. Vocabulary activities can be found on page 9 of this book.

Section 1 (Chapters 1–7)

perseverance	desolate	grimaced
gestured	expanse	stifling
expelling	excavated	preposterous
deftly	perimeter	forlorn
scarcity	juvenile	spigot

Section 2 (Chapters 8–17)

predatory	scowled	paranoid
prey	fossilized	excess
upholstery	radiated	presumably
intensity	appropriate	etched
stationery	engraved	evict

Section 3 (Chapters 18–28)

calloused	concoctions	systematic
writhed	refuge	situated
defiance	condemned	precipice
venom	recede	increments
extraordinarily	penetrating	dread

Section 4 (Chapters 29–39)

humid	jut	refuge
drenched	hesitated	fidgeting
horizon	feeble	lurched
delirious	investigation	mirage
depriving	cluster	protruding

Section 5 (Chapters 40–50)

contritely	authenticated	pursuant
inexplicable	commotion	legitimate
distinctive	amid	evicted
adjacent	precarious	incarcerated
pronounced	jurisdiction	delirium

Vocabulary Activities

You can help your students learn and retain the vocabulary in *Holes* by providing them with engaging vocabulary activities.

Here are a few to try.

1. Everyone enjoys puzzles. Ask your students to make their own word search puzzles or crossword puzzles using vocabulary from the novel.

2. Challenge your students to a vocabulary bee! This is similar to a spelling bee, but in addition to spelling each word correctly, the students must give the correct definition.

3. Engage students in a contest of listening and observation. When a student uses a vocabulary word during class, write down the word, who used it, and what was said. The student who uses the largest number of vocabulary words correctly in the discussion wins the contest. Also reward a prize to the student who recognizes and notes the most vocabulary words.

4. Have students create an Illustrated Dictionary of Vocabulary Words for this unit. Assign each student a word. Students define their words on blank pages of standard size white paper. The students then add artwork to illustrate their words. Bind all pages together for a class dictionary.

5. Have students play Vocabulary Pictionary. Select one student to artistically present the first vocabulary word on the chalkboard or dry-erase board. Provide the presenter with a card displaying the word and definition. Students raise their hands to guess the word. If a student guesses correctly, he or she becomes the presenter.

6. Play Password. Divide the class into two teams. Pick one person from each team to sit facing away from the board. Write a vocabulary word on the board for the other team members to see. Teams should alternate giving one-word clues until their teammate guesses the word. Allow a 30-second time limit for responses. Select a new set of players for each vocabulary word.

7. Play Vocabulary Concentration. The goal of this game is to match vocabulary words with their definitions. Have students get into groups of 2–4. Students should make two sets of cards the same color and size. On one set of cards write the vocabulary words, and on the other set write the definitions. All the cards are shuffled and placed facedown on the table. A student picks two cards. If the selection is a match, the student keeps the cards and takes another turn. If the cards don't match, the student turns them facedown again and the next student gets a turn. Players must be attentive to the placement of words and definitions.

8. Play Vocabulary Charades. In this game, words are acted out. Allow each student to take a turn presenting. Give a small prize to the student or team able to correctly guess the most words.

9. Have students play Vocabulary Categories, a game in which they create a chart by sorting vocabulary words into the following categories: nouns, verbs, adjectives, and adverbs. After the words are listed on the chart, discuss how words often have multiple meanings and how a reader can tell which meaning a word has by the context in which it is used.

Quiz Time!

Use complete sentences to answer the following questions about chapters 1 through 7.

1. What is the worst thing that can happen to you at Camp Green Lake? _____

_____

_____

2. What choice does the judge give Stanley? _____

_____

_____

3. What does Stanley learn that he will be doing everyday? _____

_____

_____

4. Why are there no guard towers or electric fences at the camp? _____

_____

_____

5. What is the most important rule at Camp Green Lake? _____

_____

_____

6. What does Stanley determine a nickname indicates? _____

_____

7. Why does Stanley lie about stealing the sneakers? _____

_____

_____

_____

8. What does Stanley think when the sneakers fall on his head? _____

_____

_____

9. According to Mr. Pendanski, why are the boys digging holes every day? _____

_____

_____

10. When each boy finishes digging his hole, what is the ritual he does? _____

_____

_____

Make a Model of Camp Green Lake

Have you ever read or heard about a place and later visited it? When you got there, did it look different than you expected? Having a picture or model to look at can help you better understand a place or event about which you are learning.

To better understand the story in *Holes*, work as a class to create a model of Camp Green Lake. In a model, size is very important. Each piece of the model should be sized appropriately in relation to the other pieces. For example, the figure of a person would not be the same height as a building. You should also try to make your details as realistic as possible. Pay close attention to details given in the story, such as placement, color, size, and labeling.

As a class, brainstorm about the various aspects of Camp Green Lake that should be included in the model. Write these on the board as you go. Discuss the appropriate size for the model.

After the basic parts for your model have been identified, divide the class into groups. Each group should take responsibility for a specific part or parts of the model. With your group, identify specific details to be included for your part(s). Determine what materials would be needed to construct them. Try to come up with materials that are easily available at home or school such as wood scraps, milk cartons, fabric scraps, paper bags, cardboard, sand, rocks, etc.

Meet together again as a whole class to discuss the project.

The teacher can let you know what materials he or she can supply. You should divide equally the responsibility for bringing other needed supplies.

Work together as a group on your part(s). Walk around the room occasionally to see what other groups are doing. This will give you construction ideas while ensuring each part is the appropriate size.

When all parts are completed, carefully put your model together.

It is best to locate it on a table or counter, if possible.

Here is an example of how parts might be assigned:

Group 1: The Warden's cabin

Group 2: The lake bed where the boys dig

Group 3: The tents

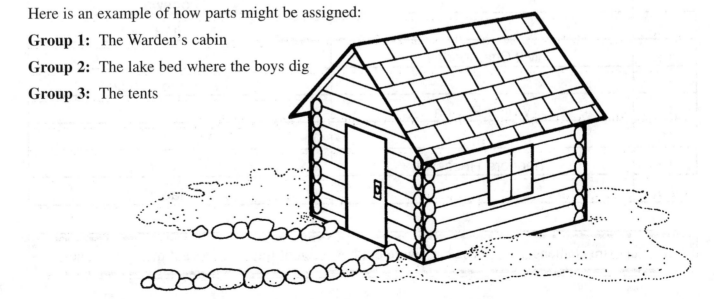

Nicknames are Nifty

In *Holes*, many of the characters have nicknames. Stanley is given the name "Caveman" for bravely standing up to a bully; Jose is nicknamed "Magnet" because "his fingers are like magnets"; and Rex's nickname, X-Ray, is from the fictitious language of pig latin. Nicknames can be a variation of someone's real name. They can also derive from people's skills, achievements, or characteristics. As Stanley observed, nicknames can also be terms of respect.

Work with a partner or in small groups to research the following people. Fill in the missing real name or nickname. Use your school library or the Internet to do the research.

	Real Name	Nickname
1.	Harriet Tubman	
2.	Dwight D. Eisenhower	
3.		"Old Hickory"
4.	Wayne Gretzsky	
5.	Edwin Aldrin	
6.	Zachary Taylor	
7.		"Honest Abe"
8.		"The Refrigerator"
9.	Frank Sinatra	
10.		"The King of Rock 'n' Roll"
11.		"The Babe"
12.	Julius Erving	
13.		"Stonewall"
14.		"FDR"
15.	Wilt Chamberlain	
16.		"Lemonade Lucy"
17.	Walter Payton	
18.		"Mr. October"
19.	Theodore Roosevelt	
20.		"Magic"

For an extra challenge, see if you can figure out how each of these people got their nicknames!

What's West Texas Really Like?

In *Holes*, Camp Green Lake is in West Texas—but what is West Texas really like? Louis Sachar describes a desolate, barren, desert-like environment with little greenery and even less water. This could accurately describe parts of West Texas, a geographic area where it is common to experience months without rain and the recorded high temperature is 120°F (54°C). Few plants are hardy enough to survive in this environment!

Using a Texas or United States map, locate the western area of Texas. Once you have an idea of location, review these statistics about the area:

- ❑ Highest recorded temperature: 120°F (54°C)

- ❑ Average annual rainfall: 8"–10" (20 cm–25 cm)

- ❑ Natural vegetation includes various hardy grasses, mesquite trees, and a variety of cacti.

- ❑ The geography is very diverse, ranging from flat plains to canyons to mountain peaks of more than 8,000 feet (2.4 km) high.

- ❑ Potentially dangerous animals include cougars, rattlesnakes, and scorpions.

Use magazines and/or the Internet to collect pictures that show or represent these West Texas features. Now research the place you live. How does your area compare to West Texas? Write a paragraph describing the similarities and differences between West Texas and where you live.

_____

_____

_____

_____

_____

_____

_____

_____

_____

_____

_____

Use the pictures that you collected to create a class collage about West Texas. Use the collage to develop a mental picture of what Stanley was seeing at Camp Green Lake!

Reading Response Journals

One great way to ensure that the reading of *Holes* becomes a personal experience for each student is to include the use of Reading Response Journals in your plans. In these journals, the students are encouraged to respond to the story in a number of ways. Here are a few ideas:

- Tell the students that the purpose of the journal is to record their thoughts, ideas, observations, and questions as they read *Holes*.

- Provide students with or ask them to suggest topics from the story that would stimulate writing. Here are a few examples from the chapters in Section 1:

  — Stanley doesn't have many friends in school because he is overweight. Should weight be a factor in the friends you choose? Explain your answer.

  — The main rule at Camp Green Lake is not to upset the Warden. What is the main rule in your home? Why are rules important?

  — Stanley is pleased when he discovers he has been given the nickname, "Caveman." It means the boys finally respect him. Write a short paragraph telling how to earn and keep respect.

- After reading each section of the novel, students can write about events that took place in that section and their responses to those events.

- Tell students they may want to use their journals as a diary Stanley might have written at camp.

- Encourage students to create songs, ballads, skits, or poems about the novel and its characters.

- Ask students to draw a time line of the main events in their journals.

- Give students quotes from the novel and ask them to write their own responses. Make sure to do this before you go over the quotations in class. In groups, students can list the different ways people can respond to the same quote.

It is a good idea to let the students write in their journals daily. These will be read by the teacher, but no corrections or letter grade will be made. Students might be graded on completion and effort.

Note: Non-judgemental teacher notations should be made as you read the journals to let the students know you are reading and enjoying their journals. Here are some examples of responses that will please your students and encourage them to write more.

- ❏ "I like the way you use details in your explanation."
- ❏ "Nice work relating your personal experience to the story."
- ❏ "You did a great job getting into the character's head and relating to his feelings."

Quiz Time

Use complete sentences to answer the following questions about chapters 8 through 17.

1. Describe the yellow-spotted lizard. _____

   _____

   _____

2. Why do Armpit and X-Ray decide Caveman is tough? _____

   _____

   _____

3. Why does Stanley lie about Camp Green Lake when writing to his mother? _____

   _____

   _____

4. What is the first thing Stanley finds as he is digging? _____

   _____

   _____

5. What does X-Ray ask Caveman to do the next time he finds something? _____

   _____

   _____

6. Which of the boys is the understood leader? How do you know this? _____

   _____

   _____

7. What does Magnet say he wants to do when he is an adult? _____

   _____

   _____

8. What does Stanley find next? _____

   _____

   _____

9. How does giving X-Ray his second "find" affect his status with the boys?_____

   _____

   _____

10. How does Zigzag release his anger toward Stanley? _____

   _____

   _____

Camp Green Lake T-Shirts

If you've ever been to a summer camp before, you probably came back with a T-shirt. Create a catchy slogan to represent Camp Green Lake and add appropriate artwork. Transfer it onto a plain white T-shirt.

Materials

- plain T-shirt (white works best)
- scissors
- cardboard
- poster board or large piece of paper

You may also need some or all of the following to create your design:

- permanent markers
- paint pens
- fabric paint
- fabric glue
- glitter
- yarn
- assorted buttons
- colorful fabric scraps

Instructions

1. Gather all materials.

2. Use poster board or paper to practice your design. Lay out materials first before gluing.

3. Before painting your T-shirt, place cardboard inside to prevent colors from bleeding through.

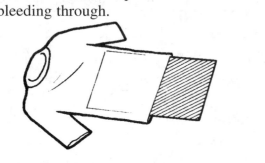

4. Allow front side to dry completely before beginning the back.

For the best presentation, be sure your design and slogan are centered or placed appropriately and that the writing is not too small.

Quiz Time

Use complete sentences to answer the following questions about chapters 8 through 17.

1. Describe the yellow-spotted lizard. _____

_____

_____

2. Why do Armpit and X-Ray decide Caveman is tough? _____

_____

_____

3. Why does Stanley lie about Camp Green Lake when writing to his mother? _____

_____

_____

4. What is the first thing Stanley finds as he is digging? _____

_____

_____

5. What does X-Ray ask Caveman to do the next time he finds something? _____

_____

_____

6. Which of the boys is the understood leader? How do you know this? _____

_____

_____

7. What does Magnet say he wants to do when he is an adult? _____

_____

_____

8. What does Stanley find next? _____

_____

_____

9. How does giving X-Ray his second "find" affect his status with the boys?_____

_____

_____

10. How does Zigzag release his anger toward Stanley? _____

_____

_____

Inventions and Their Creators

In *Holes*, Stanley's father is trying to become rich by inventing a way to recycle old sneakers. All Stanley has noticed is the terrible smell of burning rubber. Let's take a look at some inventions that were truly successful. With a partner, use your school library or the Internet to research these inventions.

Fill in the missing creator or date.

Invention	Date	Creator
vulcanization of rubber		Charles Goodyear
diapers		Maria Allen
water thermometer	1593	
bicycle		Baron Karl von Drais
airplane		Wright Brothers
telephone	1876	
zipper	1893	
air conditioning		W.H. Carrier
aspirin		Charles Gerhardt
cotton gin	1793	
sewing machine (modern)	1846	
motion picture		Eadward Muybridge
projector (kinetoscope)	1893	
jeans		Levi Strauss
Band-aids		Earle Dickson

On your own or with your partner, come up with something you would like to invent. Describe your invention. What does it do? How does it work? Remember, to be successful, an invention must be practical, useful, and serve a specific purpose. Good luck!

_____

_____

_____

_____

_____

Take turns presenting your inventions to the entire class. Vote on the best one!

Fossils

While digging, Stanley discovered a fish fossil in his hole. He was very excited and thought he had found his "miracle," something that would save him from digging. Mr. Pendanski laughed and said the Warden wasn't interested in fossils. Actually, fossils are very valuable. They are our window into the past. Fossils are the remains of plants and animals that lived millions of years ago. If it weren't for fossils, we wouldn't even know that dinosaurs existed before our time. The term *fossils* comes from a Latin word that literally means "something dug up." Fossils are formed when layers of sand and mud settle over the bodies of dead animals. Over time, the hard parts—the bones, teeth, scales or shells—of the animals are turned into rock-hard minerals as the sand or mud turns to rock. Fossils can also be of something that an animal made, like a footprint, an egg, or a burrow. Sometimes the whole animal is preserved. Fossils are found in many areas around the world. Many are found in desolate areas, along back roads and highways. Some are found in rock quarries. Many may never be found as they erode with wind, ice, and waves from the ocean.

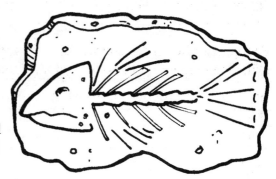

Making Your Own Fossils

Materials

- one ball of clay (per student)
- 6" x 2" (15 cm x 5 cm) strip of tagboard (per student)
- objects to imprint in the clay (shells, rocks, leaves, etc.)
- one 5-pound (2.3 kg) box of plaster of Paris
- a container and wooden spoon (to mix the plaster)

Directions

Each student will be given a ball of clay and a strip 6" x 2" (15 cm x 5 cm) of tag board (stapled into a circle). The student will role the clay out into a thickness of not less than 1". Students will press a paper ring into the clay to form a mold. Students will select the objects they wish to make into a fossil and press them into the clay. When the students carefully remove the objects, imprints are left. Fill the molds with plaster of Paris. Let them dry overnight and carefully remove the completed fossils the next day.

Caution!: Plaster of Paris hardens quickly. Be careful not to spill on working surfaces. Clean up any spills immediately.

Your Future Plans

In Chapter 12, Mr. Pendanski talks with the boys in Group D about their future plans. Mr. Pendanski emphasizes that it is important to have goals. He points out that we only have one life and that we should make the most of it. Magnet mentions his interest in animals and the possibility of a career as an animal trainer. Have you ever thought about what you would like to do as an adult? Use this activity to explore your own possible career goals and establish a plan to achieve those goals.

People are often more successful and happy at their jobs if the job relates to their interests and/or uses skills they already possess. What are some of your interests and/or skills?

Brainstorm with a partner or parent to identify five possible careers that would fit your interests and skills.

1. _____

2. _____

3. _____

4. _____

5. _____

Choose one career that most appeals to you and research it, using the library or Internet to answer these questions:

❏ What education do I need for this career (high school, college, specialized training)? _____

_____

❏ What specific tasks will my job involve? _____

_____

_____

❏ What specific skills will I need for my job? _____

_____

_____

❏ How long will it take to reach my career goal? _____

_____

On a separate piece of paper, write a paragraph describing your career goal and your plans to achieve it.

Extension Activity: Take turns helping the class guess your career goal. Using information from your research or your paragraph, give classmates one clue at a time. See how many clues your classmates will need to determine your career!

Quiz Time

Use complete sentences to answer the following questions about chapters 18 through 28.

1. What does Zero want Stanley to teach him to do? _____

    _____

2. When Stanley is sent to the Warden for stealing sunflower seeds, what does she do to him?_____

    _____

    _____

3. In what school subject does Zero excel?_____

    _____

4. After the Warden punishes Mr. Sir, how does he get even with Stanley?_____

    _____

5. What did Hattie Parker see? _____

    _____

6. Why does the sheriff want Sam to hang? _____

    _____

7. How does Sam die? _____

    _____

8. Why does Stanley save his strength during the day? _____

    _____

9. Why won't Stanley drink from his canteen?_____

    _____

    _____

10. Why does Trout threaten to kill Kate Barlow? _____

    _____

    _____

Spiced Peaches

In Chapter 23, we learn there were many peach trees growing on the shores of Green Lake. Kate Barlow was famous for her spiced peaches. She always won a special prize at the Fourth of July picnic. "It was said that Green Lake was 'heaven on Earth' and that Miss Katherine's spiced peaches were 'food for the angels.'" Later, Zero was able to stay alive by eating the 100-year-old peaches he found.

The following is a recipe for spiced peaches:

Ingredients

- 5 cups (1.2 L) brown sugar
- 6 inches (15 cm) of stick cinnamon
- pinch of nutmeg
- 2 cups (480 mL) white vinegar
- 2 tablespoons (30 mL) whole cloves
- 4 quarts (3.8 L) peeled whole peaches

Instructions

Cook sugar, vinegar, and spices over low heat for 20 minutes. Carefully drop in peaches one at a time and cook them until they are tender. Pack boiling hot peaches into hot, sterilized jars, adding boiling syrup to within ½ inch of the top. Seal jars immediately. This recipe makes 6 pints.

With your parent's assistance, find or make up your own recipe using peaches. Prepare a "how-to" presentation to instruct your classmates step-by-step how to create your dish. Prepare the dish in advance at home and bring samples for the class. Remember that you will be giving directions on preparing something that others may be unfamiliar with. It is important that your presentation includes every step of the process and explains all instructions clearly. Enjoy your classmates presentations and peach goodies!

As an extension activity, recruit outside volunteers to judge the peach dishes and award 1st, 2nd, and 3rd place ribbons!

Cause and Effect

Understanding cause-and-effect relationships is important to complete comprehension when reading. Look at the examples of cause-and-effect relationships below, then work with a partner to match the causes and effects from *Holes*.

Examples of Cause and Effect

Cause	Effect
The student studied very hard.	The student earned an A on the test.
The student did not study.	The student failed the test.

Causes

_____ 1. Magnet steals Mr. Sir's sunflower seeds.

_____ 2. The Warden scratches Mr. Sir.

_____ 3. Stanley agrees to teach Zero to read.

_____ 4. Stanley's great-great grandfather forgot to honor a promise.

_____ 5. Stanley was caught with stolen shoes.

_____ 6. Stanley gives X-Ray the gold tube he finds.

_____ 7. Stanley is overweight.

_____ 8. Stanley does not want his mother to worry.

_____ 9. Zero digs part of Stanley's hole each day.

_____ 10. Stanley digs a hole every day.

Effects

A. Mr. Sir does not give Stanley any water.

B. Stanley is sent to Camp Green Lake.

C. Stanley does not have many friends.

D. Stanley writes home about swimming and water skiing.

E. Stanley's family is cursed with bad luck.

F. The other boys in Group D harass Stanley.

G. Stanley is taken to see the Warden.

H. Stanley moves up a place in the water line.

I. Stanley and Zero become friends.

J. Stanley becomes stronger.

Are You a Math Whiz?

You learned in Chapter 22 that even though Zero cannot read, he is something of a math whiz. He is able to quickly calculate numbers by adding, multiplying, and dividing in his head. How good are you at math?

Without using a calculator, work with a partner to figure out the following problems. Taking turns, one person works the problem while the other person uses the second hand on a watch or clock to check how long it takes to work each problem. The timer should not look at the problems until it is his or her turn. Use a separate piece of paper for scratch work, if needed.

Write down your time next to each problem. At the end of the activity, check your answers with the teacher. Then, compare your times with those of your classmates. Who had the best times on questions answered correctly? Who are the math whizzes in your class?

1. Katherine Barlow made 30 jars of spiced peaches. She gave 12 to Sam and ate 2. She sold 5 jars to Doc Hawthorne. She accidentally dropped 1 on the floor and broke it. How many did she have left?

   Answer: _____

   Time: _____

2. Magnet ate 40 sunflower seeds. Armpit ate 35. X-Ray ate 58 seeds, but Zigzag only ate 18. If there are 200 seeds to begin with, how many were left?

   Answer: _____

   Time: _____

3. If it took Stanley 5 hours and 30 minutes to dig a hole, how many seconds did it take him?

   Answer: _____

   Time: _____

4. If Stanley was sentenced to Camp Green Lake for 18 months—from August 1st, 1997, through January 31, 1999—how many days would he be at Camp Green Lake?

   Answer: _____

   Time: _____

5. Stanley had to dig one hole every day, including Saturdays and Sundays. After 6 weeks at Camp Green Lake, how many holes had Stanley dug?

   Answer: _____

   Time: _____

Illiteracy in America

In *Holes*, we learn that Zero cannot read or write. As a homeless child, growing up on the street, he probably did not have the opportunity for formal education.

According to an extensive U.S. Department of Education study done in 1993, 23% of American adults are functionally illiterate. In other words, 40–44 million adults in our country cannot read and write well enough to perform the simplest tasks such as filling out a job application or understanding instructions on their child's medicine bottle.

According to the U.S. Department of Education, the high number of illiterate adults in our country puts the next generation of children at risk. Children of illiterate parents are much more likely to be unable to read than kids whose parents serve as reading role models.

Conduct an inner/outer circle discussion using either the questions at the bottom of this page or ones you've come up with on your own. In this type of discussion, the class is divided into two groups. The first group forms a close, tight circle in the middle of the room. The other group forms a larger circle around them. The inner circle is presented with a question to discuss. Each member of the group must contribute to the discussion in some original way during the time allowed. Time can be 5–15 minutes depending on group size and total time available for the activity. During the discussion, the other group must be completely silent.

After the time is up, the groups switch positions and the second group (now the inner group) is presented with a new question.

This continues until all questions have been discussed. This activity encourages students to explore their own opinions, exposes them to a variety of viewpoints, teaches listening skills, and promotes tolerance for different ideas.

Discussion Questions

1. What are some possible reasons some adults cannot read and write?

2. What are some things you would not be able to do if you were illiterate?

3. How does a high rate of adult illiteracy affect our entire country?

4. How could being illiterate be dangerous to your safety?

5. What are some things you can do to promote literacy in your community?

6. What steps would you follow if you were teaching someone to read?

Quiz Time

Answer the following questions about chapters 29–39 in complete sentences.

1. Why do the boys give Stanley a hard time about being "better" than them? _____

   _____

   _____

2. What does Mr. Pendaski do about the boys harassing Stanley? _____

   _____

   _____

3. Why does Zero hit Mr. Pendanski with the shovel? _____

   _____

   _____

   _____

4. Why does Stanley drive off in the water truck? _____

   _____

   _____

5. Where does Stanley find Zero? _____

   _____

   _____

6. What does Stanley plan to tell the Warden to ease their sentence upon returning? _____

   _____

   _____

7. Where do Stanley and Zero decide to go?_____

   _____

8. What is Stanley's warning to Zero?_____

   _____

   _____

9. How do the boys distract themselves from their hunger and pain? _____

   _____

   _____

10. When Zero collapses, what does Stanley do? _____

   _____

   _____

Create a Brochure

Imagine that Camp Green Lake is a typical camp. The people who run the camp would probably want to advertise in some way. Keeping in mind what Camp Green Lake is really like, design a brochure to advertise the camp. Your brochure could be realistic and serious, telling parents what their children will experience if sentenced to Camp Green Lake. It could be persuasive, trying to encourage judges throughout Texas to send boys to the camp. It could be humorous, a parody of a fun summer camp.

Most real camp brochures include information about location, organized activities, skills that campers will learn, sleeping/eating/bathing facilities, and any special features. A good brochure should be very informative and colorful.

It might help you get ideas for content, layout, and design if you look at some real brochures. A variety of brochures from hotels, parks, camps, and amusement parks are available through your school and public libraries, local chamber of commerce, or state tourism bureau. These can often be ordered on the Internet.

Materials

- variety of heavy 8 ½" x 11" paper (white or colored)
- construction paper
- markers
- rulers

- scissors
- glue
- magazines (to cut pictures from)
- any other creative supplies

Instructions

1. Take one piece of heavy paper for your brochure. Turn paper horizontally so paper is longest from left to right.

2. Fold left ⅓ of paper forward towards the middle.

3. Fold right ⅓ of paper backwards toward the middle.

4. Now that you have your brochure, start writing, drawing, and pasting pictures. Create pictures by cutting them from magazines, drawing, and/or using construction paper.

5. Display the brochures on a class bulletin board.

Just the Facts, Please!

When you are reading, it is important to be able to distinguish between fact and opinion. A fact is something that can be proved or verified.

Example of a *fact:* Fish live in the ocean.

We can go into the ocean and look for the fish. We can see that they are there. An opinion is something that one person or group believes to be true. An opinion cannot be proven.

Example of an *opinion:* There are many beautiful fish in the ocean.

We could verify that there are fish in the ocean; however, whether or not they are beautiful is a matter of opinion. There are people who would disagree, and there is no way to prove that statement. Some key words that often indicate an opinion are *best, worst, ugly, beautiful, wrong, right, good, bad, better,* and *great.* Look for these words and others that describe something about which people could easily disagree.

See how well you are able to tell the difference between **fact** and **opinion**. Working with a group or a partner, write **F** or **O** in the blank that precedes each incident from the book.

_____ 1. Zero told the other boys it was his birthday.

_____ 2. Stanley was almost as good at digging as Zero.

_____ 3. Kate Barlow robbed Stanley's great grandfather and left him stranded in the desert.

_____ 4. Mr. Pendanski fired his gun in the air to stop the fight.

_____ 5. The boys had to dig holes because it was good for them.

_____ 6. Barf Bag deliberately stepped on a rattlesnake.

_____ 7. Onions are delicious and nutritious.

_____ 8. Stanley stepped backward, away from the lizards.

_____ 9. No one helped Stanley dig Zero's hole after he left.

_____ 10. Stanley had a good idea for himself and Zero to escape Camp Green Lake.

_____ 11. The other boys called the new kid in Group D, Twitch.

_____ 12. After awhile, Stanley's cot no longer smelled bad.

_____ 13. Mr. Sir was the toughest counselor at Camp Green Lake.

_____ 14. There were patches of weeds and swarms of bugs on the mountainside.

_____ 15. Carrying someone up a mountain is always difficult.

Have you mastered fact and opinion? Write two facts and two opinions about *Holes*.

Fact 1 _____

Fact 2 _____

Opinion 1 _____

Opinion 2 _____

Conflicts

Conflict is the struggle against an obstacle or opposing force. Writers use conflict to keep you interested in reading so you can discover how the situation or conflict turns out. Conflict can be broken down into six types.

> **A. Person vs. Self**—The character faces a struggle against his own emotions, conscience, or physical abilities.
> Example: A teen struggles over whether to report a classmate he saw cheating.
>
> **B. Person vs. Person**—The character struggles against another character.
> Example: A girl dares another girl to steal something.
>
> **C. Person vs. Society**—The character struggles against something presented by society or a representative of society.
> Example: A convicted man appeals a jury's verdict he feels is unfair.
>
> **D. Person vs. Nature**—The character struggles against a force of nature.
> Example: A man's house is blown away in the hurricane.
>
> **E. Person vs. Unknown**—The character struggles against an unknown force.
> Example: He was scared by strange sounds in the attic.
>
> **F. Person vs. Machine**—The character struggles against a machine or tool.
> Example: A computer deletes your entire report.

Read the following situations from *Holes* and determine which type of conflict is presented. Write the corresponding letter on the line provided.

_____ 1. Stanley was often teased by other kids because he was overweight.

_____ 2. Stanley was convicted of a crime he did not commit.

_____ 3. The boys knew that the longer it took to dig their holes, the longer they would be out in the sun's heat.

_____ 4. Armpit shoves Stanley to the ground for calling him by his real name, Theodore.

_____ 5. At first, Stanley's hands are blistered and bloody from digging with the shovel.

_____ 6. Elya was in love with Myra Menke, but he could not compete with Igor's offer of his fattest pig.

_____ 7. Elya told his wife, Sarah, that she should leave him because he was cursed.

_____ 8. Stanley tried to pull himself out of his hole, but he was too exhausted.

_____ 9. Stanley talks back when another boy confronts him in the "Wreck Room."

_____ 10. Stanley believed that they were not digging to build character. He felt they were digging to find something; he just did not know what.

Bullies

In *Holes*, there are several situations which involve bullies. For instance, Stanley describes Derrick Dunne, the bully at his middle school. Derrick stole Stanley's notebook and put it in the toilet. Stanley continues to be bullied at Camp Green Lake by X-Ray, who pressures him to turn over his valuable find. He is also bullied by Zigzag, who is angry about Zero digging Stanley's hole. A less obvious bully is Mr. Pendanski. He antagonizes and puts down Zero. Mr. Pendanski calls him stupid and qualified only to dig holes. He also makes fun of Zero's struggling attempts to learn to read.

Most people will encounter bullies in their lifetimes. If you have not already, you probably will. How will you react? Will you be able to handle the situation? As a class, brainstorm about the best ways to deal with bullies.

Divide into size-appropriate groups to discuss and plan your responses and/or actions in the following scenarios. Act out your scenarios for the class.

Scenarios

1. A large student with a reputation for meanness catches you alone in the bathroom at school. He threatens to beat you up if you do not pay him $5.00.

2. Another student in your class wants to copy off your paper during a test. He threatens to spread false rumors about you if you do not let him.

3. A popular girl offers you drugs. When you decline, she makes fun of you and says you will never be popular.

4. A coach often makes fun of you and/or other students who are not athletically gifted.

5. A student who is a grade above you has a locker above yours. He is always blocking your locker until the last minute, intentionally making you late for class.

6. You and your friends are playing basketball in the park. A group of older kids arrive and take over the court.

Quiz Time

Use complete sentences to answer the following questions about chapters 40 through 50.

1. What does Zero confess to Stanley? _____

   _____

2. Why didn't Zero know the shoes he took belonged to Clyde Livingston?_____

   _____

3. Why does Stanley decide he is glad the shoes hit him on the head? _____

   _____

   _____

4. As the two boys make their way down the mountain, what is the unspoken challenge between
   them? _____

   _____

5. After returning to the hole where Stanley found the lipstick tube, what do the boys uncover?_____

   _____

6. What does Mr. Sir reveal to Stanley about his guilt? _____

   _____

7. Why doesn't Stanley want to leave camp when he is released? _____

   _____

8. Why does Stanley's attorney take Zero with them when they leave?_____

   _____

9. Why aren't Stanley and Zero attacked by the yellow-spotted lizards?_____

   _____

   _____

10. How does the author account for the sudden success of Stanley's father?_____

   _____

Who's on Trial?

Have you ever been in a courtroom or watched a movie about someone accused of a crime? This is an important part of our society, the process of trying people accused of crimes and giving appropriate punishment for those found guilty.

As American citizens, we are guaranteed certain rights and protections under the law if we are accused of a crime. We are innocent until proven guilty in a court of law. We have the right to a trial by a jury of our peers. We have the right to be represented by a lawyer. We also have the right to remain silent if what we are being asked might be used against us to prove we are guilty ("taking the 5th"—exercising your 5th Amendment privileges).

In a criminal trial, you will usually find the following people:

Judge—He or she oversees the entire trial. The judge makes sure everyone follows the rules in court. If someone is found guilty, the judge is often the one who decides the punishment.

Jury—This is made up of 12 people who will hear all the evidence and then decide if the defendant is guilty or innocent.

Defendant—This is the person accused of the crime.

Defense attorney—This is the lawyer who tries to prove that the defendant is not guilty. If guilt is obvious, the defense attorney will try to convince the jury that there was a good reason for the crime or that the defendant is insane.

Prosecutor—This the lawyer who tries to prove the defendant is guilty.

Witness(es)—Both the Defense Attorney and the Prosecutor ask the witnesses questions in the hopes of persuading the jury to believe what they want to prove. The defense attorney and the prosecutor ask the witnesses questions which they must answer honestly.

Use this information to conduct a mock trial of scenarios below, based on events in *Holes*. The entire class should participate, using the roles listed above. Think about the following when planning:

❏ What witnesses will each lawyer call to testify?

❏ What questions will each lawyer ask the witnesses? (Remember, both lawyers have the right to ask all of the witnesses questions.)

❏ What evidence will be presented? (weapons, clothing, pictures, diagrams, or anything else that will prove their case)

❏ Will the defendant testify?

❏ If guilty, what would be an appropriate punishment?

Choose one of these scenarios or come up with your own:

1. The Warden is charged with neglect and abuse of the boys in her custody.

2. Zero is charged with stealing Clyde Livingston's shoes.

3. Zero is charged with assaulting Mr. Pendanski.

What a Character!

In order to give depth to a story and increase reader involvement, authors use characterization, which means they provide details that describe a character and make that character seem more real. Characterization can include physical descriptions, such as "has blue eyes"; "has long, brown hair"; "is tall"; and "wears hats." It can also include personality traits such as "mean," "generous," "happy," "kind," and "short tempered." Characterization even describes skills, habits, and the person's strengths and weaknesses. This could include such descriptions as "steals," "fights often," "speed-reads," "has nervous twitches," "is an insomniac," and/or "speaks well in public."

The examples given above are only a few of the almost endless character descriptions that an author may use to bring his characters to life for the reader. Remember, anything that identifies a character's appearance, feelings, personality, or actions could be called characterization.

Complete the following chart about the characters from *Holes*.

Character (real name)	Nickname	Description
Stanley		
Mr. Pendanski		
	The Warden	
	X-Ray	
	Armpit	
	Squid	
	Magnet	
	Zigzag	
	Zero	

Understanding Point of View

In many situations you might encounter, you will only be presented with one point of view. For example, if a good friend told you that a movie she went to see was terrible and recommended that you not see it, you probably would listen to her and never see the movie. However, there are certainly different points of view about the movie. If you asked other people who had seen it, you would probably find someone who thought it was great.

In any situation, people are going to have different points of view about what has happened, what is happening, and what should happen. In *Holes*, the story is presented from Stanley's point of view. As readers, we are given a firsthand account of how he feels about what is happening and how he views the events. What about other points of view? Using complete sentences, explore some different viewpoints in the following activity. Use the back of this page or a separate sheet of paper for your writing.

- In chapters 45–48, Stanley and Zero discover the suitcase, are descended upon by the Warden and the lizards, are rescued by Stanley's lawyer and the Attorney General, and leave Camp Green Lake with the suitcase. Write a possible entry the Warden might make in her diary describing the day's events. Remember that you are writing from her point of view.

- In chapters 45–47, Stanley is standing in a lizard's nest. The author describes what he is feeling and how he escapes mentally in order to handle the situation. Write an imaginary conversation between Zero and Stanley after this incident. In the conversation, Zero should tell Stanley what he was feeling during the time and how he coped with the situation. Remember that you are writing from Zero's point of view.

- In chapter 49, we learn that on the very same day that Stanley carries Zero up the mountain Stanley's father invents a cure for foot odor. Write a monologue (a one-person speech) in which Stanley's father ponders his possible change of fortune. Remember, things have happened to the Yelnats before which seem positive at first but turn negative in the end.

- Throughout *Holes*, there is mention of Clyde "Sweet Feet" Livingston's foot-odor problem. Write a letter from Clyde to his personal physician, which details the problem and explains what it is like to be famous and to have an embarrassing secret. Remember that you are writing from Clyde's point of view.

- Pretend you are either Mr. Sir or Mr. Pendanski and you are submitting an article on the United States justice system to a local newspaper. Write an editorial describing your views on children who commit crimes and how those children should be punished. Remember that you are writing from either Mr. Sir's or Mr. Pendanski's point of view.

Extension: Volunteers can share their writings with the class or present their conversation with a partner.

Homelessness in America

In *Holes*, you are presented with the fact that before coming to Camp Green Lake, Zero was homeless. In conversations with Stanley, he reveals that he was not always homeless. What does it really mean to be homeless? What are some possible reasons that Zero or real people in your community end up homeless? Take this quiz before reading the information below:

1. People choose to be homeless.   **Agree   Disagree**

2. Homeless people are drug addicts.   **Agree   Disagree**

3. Homeless people are adults.   **Agree   Disagree**

4. People are homeless because they are poor and have no education. **Agree   Disagree**

5. Homeless people are criminals.   **Agree   Disagree**

In your lifetime, there has always been a condition known as homelessness. This condition effects thousands or even millions of Americans at one time or another. It is only in the last 20 years that this problem has surfaced in our country.

Today, some people estimate that as many as two million people could experience homelessness in the United States during a year. Homelessness means that they have nowhere to live, no house, no apartment, no shelter. They sleep on the street; in abandoned buildings; or, if they are lucky, in a shelter.

Homelessness can happen for a variety of reasons. Maybe the person is running from an abusive situation at home. They might be mentally ill or have a substance abuse problem. It is possible that they simply lost their job, became seriously ill, or lost everything in a fire. Homelessness has a variety of causes and it affects every kind of person. Men, women, children, young, old, black, and white can all fall victim.

Most people agree that to end homelessness, there must be affordable housing for all people. Homeless Americans must receive job training to improve their earning potential, and services must be available to assist those with mental illness or substance abuse problems. You may not realize it, but there are probably homeless people living in your community. After reading this information, would you change any answers on the quiz? Discuss this information with the class.

Accept the challenge to find out how homelessness affects your community and what you can do to help. Write a letter to your mayor, town council, state representative, or congressperson.

Think about these questions when writing your letter:

❑ What is the situation in my community?

❑ What programs are currently available to help?

❑ What can I do to help?

❑ What can my class or school do to help?

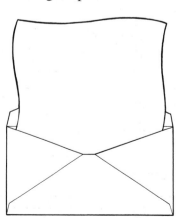

Find the Main Idea

Louis Sachar did not include titles for his chapters in *Holes*. Go back and review each of the following chapters and come up with titles. Make your titles as creative or catchy as possible, but be sure each reflects the main idea! In the space provided, use specific examples from the book to explain why you chose a particular title.

Chapter 1

Title _____

Why? _____

_____

Chapter 2

Title _____

Why? _____

_____

Chapter 8

Title _____

Why? _____

_____

Chapter 13

Title _____

Why? _____

_____

Chapter 25

Title _____

Why? _____

_____

Chapter 32

Title _____

Why? _____

_____

Chapter 38

Title _____

Why? _____

_____

Chapter 42

Title _____

Why? _____

_____

What Does It Stand For?

Symbolism is a technique used by writers in which an object or idea is used to represent something other than itself. For example, the dove is often used as a symbol of peace. The following is a list of symbols used by Louis Sachar in *Holes*. Choose from the box the appropriate meaning for each symbol. Provide specific evidence from the book that supports your choice.

warning	a better life	hope
missing pieces	obstacles	layers of history

1. Rattlesnake tattoo
   Meaning: _____
   Evidence: _____
   _____

2. Holes
   Meaning: _____
   Evidence: _____
   _____

3. Onion
   Meaning: _____
   Evidence: _____
   _____

4. Mountains
   Meaning: _____
   Evidence: _____
   _____

5. Big Thumb
   Meaning: _____
   Evidence: _____
   _____

6. Hot Fudge Sundae
   Meaning: _____
   Evidence: _____
   _____

That's Ironic!

Irony is the general name given to literary techniques that involve surprising, interesting, or amusing contradictions. When an event occurs that directly contradicts the expectations of the characters or reader, that is irony. Read the following quotes from *Holes*. Using complete sentences, explain what is ironic about the following quotes.

"Welcome to Camp Green Lake." (page 10) _____

_____

_____

"Nobody had believed him when he said he was innocent." (page 22) _____

_____

_____

"'I bet she was real pretty,' said Zero. 'Someone must have loved her a lot, to name a boat after her.' 'Yeah,' said Stanley. 'I bet she looked great in a bathing suit, sitting in the boat while her boyfriend rowed.'" (page 161)_____

_____

_____

"'You're not in the Girl Scouts anymore,' Mr. Sir said." (page 13)_____

_____

_____

"Clyde 'Sweet Feet' Livingston was a famous baseball player." (page 22)_____

_____

_____

_____

_____

Filling in the Holes

Holes could be described as a puzzle book. The author builds several different storylines that eventually come together. Did you make all the connections? Complete this activity to be sure. Fill in the missing information.

1. Elya Yelnats is Stanley's _____.

2. The suitcase belonging to the first Stanley Yelnats was in the lake because _____

   _____.

3. The "sploosh' that Zero found in the desert was really _____.

4. The woman with Zero at the end of the book is_____.

5. There were onions on top of Big Thumb because _____.

6. When Stanley carried Zero up the mountain, it broke his family's curse because _____

   _____.

7. The Warden is a descendant of _____.

8. Stanley and Zero's family lullabies were similar because _____

   _____.

9. The lizards did not bite Stanley and Zero because_____.

10. The boat was in the middle of the lake bed because _____

    _____.

Discuss your answers as a class. Point out specific evidence from the book that helped you make the connections.

Book Project Ideas

After reading *Holes*, choose one of these project ideas to explore ideas in the book and further your understanding.

A Camp Newsletter

Create a camp newsletter for Camp Green Lake. A newsletter should have a variety of sections, explore viewpoints of the different people at Camp Green Lake, and inform its readers about events and everyday life at the camp.

A Television Talk Show

Organize a talk show with several of your classmates. You will need a host, guests, and an audience. The guests should be characters from *Holes*. The host should question them about events from the book. Plan carefully, rehearse, and present your show to the class.

Make It Simple!

Write a young children's version of the events in *Holes*. Create a six to eight page children's book featuring simplified text and lots of creative artwork. You might include pop-ups, pictures behind doors, or textured objects children can touch.

Journal

Choose one of the characters in *Holes* and write ten journal entries that he or she might have made describing his or her experiences.

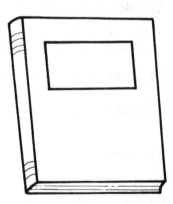

Autobiography

Assume the identity of the Warden. Write a fictional autobiography beginning with her earliest memories of childhood through what you believe happened to her after the book. You will have to make up some information, so use your imagination!

Musical Magic

Write a ballad about Stanley's experiences at Camp Green Lake. A ballad is a poem that tells a story and is often set to music. Perform your ballad for the class with or without musical accompaniment.

Cover That Book!

Create an original book jacket for *Holes*. Include artwork for the front and back, a summary in the inside front flap, and information about the author on the back inside flap. Make sure your book jacket is original and different from the actual cover.

Research Ideas

Each of the following topics was mentioned in *Holes*. Choose one that interests you and research it. Present your findings to the class.

Social Issues

❑ homelessness in your community
❑ illiteracy in your community
❑ juvenile crime
❑ juvenile prisons or detention centers
❑ innocent people convicted and sent to prison

Geography

❑ Latvia
❑ West Texas

Famous Outlaws

❑ William "Billy the Kid" Bonney
❑ Jesse James
❑ John Wesley Hardin
❑ Sam Bass
❑ Choose any outlaw that interests you!

Treasure

❑ local legends in your community about lost treasure

Genealogy

❑ your family tree and history dating back at least four generations

Famous Inventors

❑ Thomas Alva Edison
❑ Alexander Graham Bell
❑ Henry Ford
❑ Samuel Morse
❑ Louis Pasteur
❑ Eli Whitney
❑ Orville & Wilbur Wright
❑ Choose any inventor who interests you!

Conversations

In appropriately sized groups, have students write out conversations that might have taken place between characters in *Holes*. Conversations should be written in a style similar to a play or interview in which each speaker is identified. As an extension, students may act out their conversations. Use the following situations from the novel as guidelines for your conversations or come up with your own scenarios.

1. Stanley and Derrick Dunne are in the boys' bathroom the day Stanley is arrested. Derrick has Stanley's notebook. (*two persons*)

2. Mr. Pendanski and X-Ray are riding back to camp in the truck after X-Ray "finds" the gold tube. (*two persons*)

3. Stanley's parents are reading his letter from Camp Green Lake. (two persons)

4. After the Warden scratches Mr. Sir, Stanley leaves and the Warden and Mr. Sir are alone in the cabin. (*two persons*)

5. Sam and Katherine talk while Sam fixes the schoolhouse roof. (two persons)

6. The Warden, Mr. Sir, and Mr. Pendanski are waiting for Stanley in his tent when he returns from the lake. It is the day after Zero ran away. What went on before Stanley arrived? (three persons)

7. Katherine and Sam row across the lake, attempting to escape Trout Walker and the other townspeople. (*two persons*)

8. Kate Barlow robs Stanley's great-grandfather. (*two persons*)

9. The Attorney General and Ms. Walker talk in her office. (*two persons*)

10. Stanley and Zero tell Stanley's parents about their experience finding the suitcase. (*four persons*)

11. Zero and his mother are reunited. (*two persons*)

12. The Warden, Mr. Pendanski, and Mr. Sir talk after Stanley, his lawyer, and Zero left. (*three persons*)

13. Linda and Trout Walker watch Kate die without revealing the location of her loot. (*two persons*)

14. Stanley and his family persuade Clyde Livingston to endorse Sploosh. (*four persons*)

15. Stanley and his parents have a final talk before Stanley is taken to Camp Green Lake (*three persons*)

16. Elya Yelnats and his wife Sarah discuss why bad things always happen to him. (*two persons*)

17. Stanley tells his story to the judge in court, and the judge asks questions. (*two persons*)

18. Stanley's lawyer explains the contents of the suitcase to Stanley and Zero. (*three persons*)

19. Miss Katherine conducts an evening class for adults; Trout Walker is one of the students. (*four to six persons*)

20. Hattie Parker tells several other townspeople about Sam and Kate kissing. (*three to four persons*)

Objective Test and Essay

Sections 1–3

Cause and Effect: Match the cause on the left with the effect that most directly followed.

Cause

Effect

_____ 1. Magnet steals Mr. Sir's sunflower seeds.

A. Stanley goes to Camp Green Lake.

_____ 2. The Warden scratches Mr. Sir.

B. Stanley has to go see the Warden.

_____ 3. Stanley gives X-Ray the tube he found.

C. Stanley's family is cursed with bad luck.

_____ 4. Stanley is caught with stolen shoes.

D. Mr. Sir doesn't give Stanley any water.

_____ 5. Elya did not carry Mdme. Zeroni up the mountain.

E. Stanley takes Zero's place in line.

True or False: Write True or False in the blank for each statement.

_____ 6. Stanley did not have to go to Camp Green Lake.

_____ 7. Stanley's family was wealthy prior to his incarceration at Camp Green Lake.

_____ 8. Zero was the leader of the boys at Camp Green Lake.

_____ 9. Each of the boys at Camp Green Lake had to dig five holes per week.

_____ 10. X-Ray wants Stanley to teach him to read.

_____ 11. Stanley's first "find" is a fossil.

_____ 12. Sam is killed for kissing Kate.

_____ 13. Armpit helps Stanley dig his hole each day.

_____ 14. Stanley is guilty of stealing the shoes.

_____ 15. The one rule at Camp Green Lake is "Don't get bit by a lizard."

Sequencing: Place the following events in order by placing numbers 1–5 in the blanks.

_____ 16. Stanley is arrested.

_____ 17. Stanley agrees to teach Zero to read.

_____ 18. Stanley digs his first hole.

_____ 19. Stanley finds a gold tube.

_____ 20. Stanley meets Mr. Sir.

Essay: On the back of this page, describe Camp Green Lake. Use as many details as possible. Use complete sentences and write in paragraph form.

Objective Test and Essay

Sections 4 and 5

Matching: Match each character with the appropriate description.

_____ 1. overweight, mild-mannered, unlucky, hopeful	A. Mr. Pendanski
_____ 2. steals things, sneaky, does not take responsibility for his actions, Hispanic	B. Zero
_____ 3. quiet, good at math, fast learner, smallest in Group D	C. X-Ray
_____ 4. seems sympathetic, positive attitude, almost bald, curly black beard	D. Mr. Sir
_____ 5. biggest in Group D (except Stanley), overreacts, short temper, spitter	E. Stanley
_____ 6. poor vision, wears glasses, leader of the group, pushes people around	F. Magnet
_____ 7. mean, vengeful, dangerous, has a tattoo, bad temper	G. Armpit

Conflict: Identify the type of conflict presented in each situation by placing the corresponding letter in the blank. Letters can be used more than once.

Types of Conflict

A. Person vs. Self   D. Person vs. Person

B. Person vs. Society   E. Person vs. Unknown

C. Person vs. Nature   F. Person vs. Machine

_____ 8. "Stanley was not a bad kid. He was innocent of the crime for which he was convicted."

_____ 9. "The longer it takes you to dig, the longer you'll be out in the sun."

_____ 10. "He put his hands on the rim and tried to pull himself up. He couldn't do it."

_____ 11. "One thing was certain: They weren't just digging to build character. They were definitely looking for something."

_____ 12. "The shovel felt heavy in Stanley's soft fleshy hands. He tried to jam it into the earth, but the blade banged against the ground and bounced off without making a dent. The vibrations ran up the shaft of the shovel and into Stanley's wrists, making his bones rattle."

Essay: Write a paragraph which describes two examples of irony from *Holes*. Use complete sentences and explain each example fully.

What's Your Opinion?

Carefully read each of the following opinions about events in the book. Do you agree or not? Using complete sentences, state your opinion and give specific evidence from the book to support it.

Stanley did not have any friends because he was overweight. _____

_____

_____

_____

Mr. Pendanski was truly concerned about the well-being of all the boys. _____

_____

_____

_____

Stanley should have lied and said he found the shoes on the street. _____

_____

_____

_____

Camp Green Lake was a positive experience for Stanley._____

_____

_____

_____

Stanley should have kept all the money for himself. _____

_____

_____

_____

If they had met away from Camp Green Lake, Stanley and Zero would never have been friends. _____

_____

_____

_____

Stanley should not have stolen the truck because stealing is always wrong. _____

_____

_____

_____

Illustrated Plot Line

A **plot line** is the basic structure that a story follows. This is what it looks like:

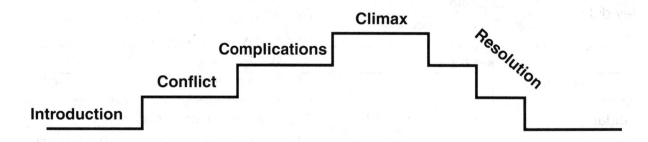

The **introduction** introduces the characters and provides the setting and any background information necessary to understand the story.

The **conflict** is a problem or problems that need to be solved.

Complications are what stand in the way of solving the conflict.

The **climax** is the highest or most exciting point of the story. In the climax, the problem is usually solved.

In the **resolution**, the reader finds out what happens after the climax. It shows how the characters act, think, and feel after the climax.

On a separate piece of paper, create an illustrated plot line. First, write an explanation about *Holes* for each of the elements: introduction, conflict, complications, climax, and resolution. Your explanations should be accurate but brief, limited to a couple of sentences each. Next, using the plot line structure above as a guideline, create your own plot line on a separate piece of paper. Do not write the name of each element. Instead, write your short explanations in the appropriate place on the line. Finally, draw an illustration for each element that corresponds with your explanation from *Holes*. Be creative and colorful!

Answer Key

Page 10

1. You can be bitten by a yellow-spotted lizard.

2. He can go to jail or to Camp Green Lake.

3. He will be digging a hole five feet deep by five feet wide.

4. Camp has the only water for 100 miles.

5. Don't upset the Warden.

6. A nickname is a term of respect.

7. He thought the other boys' crimes were probably worse, and he thought no one would believe him if he said he was innocent.

8. He thinks that it is a sign and the shoes are a gift from God.

9. Mr. Pendanski says the boys are digging to build character.

10. He spits in his hole when he is done.

Page 12

1. "Moses"

2. "Ike"

3. Andrew Jackson

4. "The Great One"

5. "Buzz"

6. "Old Rough and Ready"

7. Abraham Lincoln

8. William Perry

9. "Old Blue Eyes" or "Chairman of the Board"

10. Elvis Presley

11. George Herman Ruth

12. "Dr. J"

13. Thomas Jackson

14. Franklin Delano Roosevelt

15. "Wilt the Stilt"

16. Lucy Hayes (First Lady, wife of Rutherford B. Hayes)

17. "Sweetness"

18. Reggie Jackson

19. "Teddy"

20. Earvin Johnson

Page 15

1. It has a yellow-green body—6–10 inches in length—with exactly eleven yellow spots, black teeth, a white tongue, and red-rimmed yellow eyes.

2. Cavemen stands up to the "orange lump" in the "Wreck Room."

3. He does not want her to worry.

4. He finds a fossilized fish.

5. X-Ray wants Stanley to give him anything else he finds.

6. X-Ray is always first in the water line.

7. Magnet wants to work with animals, maybe as a monkey trainer.

8. Stanley's second find is a gold tube with the initials "K B" engraved on it.

9. Stanley moves up a place in the water line, indicating that he has moved up in the boys' ranking system.

10. He hits Stanley in the head with a shovel.

Page 17

Invention	Date	Creator
vulcanization of rubber	1839	Charles Goodyear
diapers	1887	Maria Allen
water thermometer	1593	Galileo
bicycle	1817	Baron Karl von Drais
airplane	1903	Wright Brothers
telephone	1876	Alexander Graham Bell
zipper	1893	Whitcomb Judson
air conditioning	1902	W.H. Carrier
aspirin	1853	Charles Gerhardt
cotton gin	1793	Eli Whitney
sewing machine (modern)	1846	Elias Howe
motion picture	1877	Eadward Muybridge
projector (kinetoscope)	1893	Thomas Edison
jeans	1873	Levi Strauss
Band-aids	1920	Earl Dickson

Page 20

1. Zero wants Stanley to teach him to read.

2. She gently scrapes her poisonous nails across Stanley's face. After viciously scratching Mr. Sir, she sends Stanley back to the lake.

3. Zero is very good at math.

4. Mr. Sir does not give Stanley any water when he brings the water truck out to where the boys are digging.

5. She saw Katherine and Sam kissing.

6. The sheriff wants to hang Sam because he is black and he kissed a white woman.

Answer Key (cont.)

7. Sam is shot in the water after Trout Walker rams his boat.

8. Stanley saves his strength to teach Zero.

9. Stanley is afraid of what Mr. Sir might have put in his canteen.

10. Trout threatens to kill Kate Barlow because she will not tell him where she has hidden her treasure.

Page 22

1. G	3. I	5. B	7. C	9. F
2. A	4. E	6. H	8. D	10. J

Page 23

1. 10	3. 19,800	5. 42
2. 49	4. 549	

Page 25

1. The boys give Stanley a hard time because Zero is digging part of his hole each day.

2. Mr. Pendanski encourages Stanley to hit Zigzag.

3. Zero hits Mr. Pendanski with the shovel because Mr. Pendanski is constantly putting him down and saying how stupid he is.

4. Stanley drives off with the water truck to look for Zero.

5. Stanley finds Zero under an old boat in the middle of the lake bed.

6. Stanley plans to tell the Warden where the gold tube was really found.

7. They decide to go to Big Thumb.

8. Stanley warns Zero that he is unlucky.

9. The boys distract themselves by spelling.

10. After Zero collapses, Stanley carries him up the mountain.

Page 27

1. F	4. F	7. O	10. O	13. O
2. O	5. O	8. F	11. F	14. F
3. F	6. O	9. F	12. O	15. O

Page 28

1. C	3. D	5. F	7. A	9. B
2. C	4. B	6. B	8. A	10. E

Page 30

1. Zero confesses that he stole Clyde Livingston's shoes.

2. He could not read the sign.

3. Stanley is glad the shoes hit him on the head because he is happy with himself. He has lost weight, made a good friend, and maybe it is his destiny to be at the Camp.

4. Neither boy wants to be the first one to take a drink of water.

5. Stanley and Zero uncover a suitcase.

6. Mr. Sir tells Stanley that he is innocent.

7. He doesn't want to leave without Zero.

8. Stanley's lawyer took Zero with them because no one could find his records.

9. Stanley and Zero, who have eaten many onions, are not bitten because the lizards do not like onion blood.

10. The family curse was broken after Stanley carried Zero up the mountain.

Page 42

1. B	8. False	15. False
2. D	9. False	16. 1
3. E	10. False	17. 5
4. A	11. True	18. 3
5. C	12. True	19. 4
6. True	13. False	20. 2
7. False	14. False	

Page 43

1. E	4. A	7. D	10. A
2. F	5. G	8. B	11. E
3. B	6. C	9. A, F	12. C, F

Page 44

Answers will vary.

Page 45

Answers will vary. They should indicate knowledge of book and accurate application of information about elements of plot.

Bibliography of Related Reading

Fiction

Homelessness

Bodie, Idella. *Stranded!* Sandlapper Publishing Co., Inc., 1986.

Warner, Gertrude C. *The Box Car Children*. Albert Whitman, 1989.

Carlson, Natalie S. *The Family Under the Bridge*. HarperCollins, 1989.

Creel, Ann H. *A Ceiling of Stars*. Pleasant Co., 1999

Bullies

Hahn, Mary D. *Stepping on the Cracks*. Houghton Mifflin, 1991.

Trembath, Don. *A Fly Named Alfred*. Orca Books, 1997.

Survival/Personal Challenges

Paulsen, Gary. *Brian's Winter*. Bantam Books, 1998.

Paulsen, Gary. *The River*. Bantam Doubleday, 1992.

AVI. *The True Confessions of Charlotte Doyle*. William Morrow & Co., 1992.

Golding, William G. *Lord of the Flies*. Chelsea House, 1996.

Finding Treasure

Buchanan, Paul. *Gold Flakes for Breakfast*. Concordia, 1998.

Stevenson, Robert Louis. *Treasure Island*. Bantam Books, 1978.

Schwartz, Alvin. *Gold and Silver, Silver and Gold*. Farrar, Straus & Giroux, 1993.

Texas

Gipson, Fred. *Old Yeller*. Harper Trade, 1976.

Henderson, Aileen K. *Treasure of Panther Peak*. Milkweed Editions, 1998.

Judicial Error.

Pfeiffer, Susan B. *Justice for Emily*. Bantam Doubleday, 1998.

Non-Fiction

Crime and Punishment

Lane, Brian. *Crime and Detection*. John Wiley & Sons, 1998.

Nunez, Sandra. *And Justice For All: The Legal Rights of Young People*. Millbrook, 1999.

Stewart, Gail B. *Teens in Prison*. Lucent Books, 1991.

Homelessness

Chalofsky, Margie. *Changing Faces*. Gryphon House, 1995.

Hubbard, Jim. *Lives Turned Upside Down*. Simon & Schuster, 1996.

Bullies

Doyle, Terrace W. *Why is Everybody Always Picking On Me?* Weatherhill, 1999.

Romain, Trevor. *Bullies Are a Pain in the Brain*. Free Spirit Publishing, Inc., 1997.

Finding Treasure

Marx, Robert. *Buried Treasures You Can Find*. Ram, 1995.

Illiteracy

Dolan, Edward F. *Illiteracy in America*. Watts Franklin, 1995.

Ryan, Bernard. *Expanding Education and Literacy: Opportunities to Volunteer*. Ferguson, 1998.

Texas

Texas Almanac. Dallas Morning News, 1996–1997 or 1997–1998.

Judicial Error

Sullivan, George A. *Not Guilty*. Scholastic, 1997.

Camp Green Lake T-Shirts

If you've ever been to a summer camp before, you probably came back with a T-shirt. Create a catchy slogan to represent Camp Green Lake and add appropriate artwork. Transfer it onto a plain white T-shirt.

Materials

- plain T-shirt (white works best)
- scissors
- cardboard
- poster board or large piece of paper

You may also need some or all of the following to create your design:

- permanent markers
- paint pens
- fabric paint
- fabric glue
- glitter
- yarn
- assorted buttons
- colorful fabric scraps

Instructions

1. Gather all materials.

2. Use poster board or paper to practice your design. Lay out materials first before gluing.

3. Before painting your T-shirt, place cardboard inside to prevent colors from bleeding through.

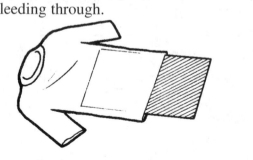

4. Allow front side to dry completely before beginning the back.

For the best presentation, be sure your design and slogan are centered or placed appropriately and that the writing is not too small.